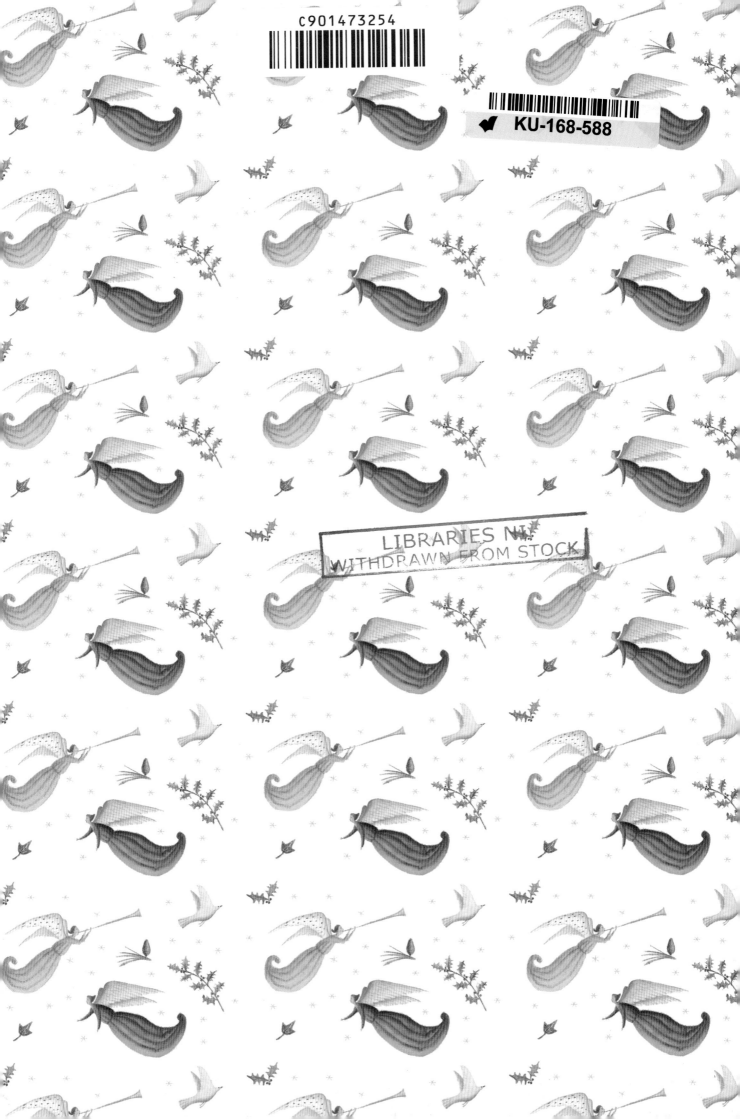

Text by Lois Rock
Illustrations copyright © 2015 Alison Jay
This edition copyright © 2015 Lion Hudson

Published by Lion Children's Books
an imprint of
Lion Hudson plc
Wilkinson House, Jordan Hill Road,
Oxford OX2 8DR, England
www.lionhudson.com/lionchildrens

ISBN 978 0 7459 6588 8

First edition 2015

A catalogue record for this book is available from the British Library

Printed and bound in Malaysia, June 2015, LH18

On That Christmas Night

LOIS ROCK

ILLUSTRATED BY ALISON JAY

LION
CHILDREN'S

I**N THE LITTLE** town of Nazareth, no one thought much about angels.

Not Joseph: the hardworking carpenter, busy in his workshop.

Nor Mary, who always smiled as she dreamed of the day when she would be Joseph's bride.

THEN, ONE DAY, the angel whose name is Gabriel was sent by God to Nazareth, with a message for Mary. "Do not be alarmed," said Gabriel. "God has chosen you to be the mother of his Son. You will name him Jesus. He will grow up to show God's love and grace to all the world."

Mary was astonished. "I can't be a mother!" she protested. "Why, I'm not even married."

"It is God who will make this all come true," replied the angel.

Mary bowed her head. "I will do as God wants," she said.

THE TOWNSFOLK OF Nazareth had not seen the angel, but they soon found out the news.

Mary was expecting a baby… and Joseph wasn't the father.

"Tut tut," and "Oh dear," they gossiped. "Whatever will the poor man do?"

In a dream, an angel spoke to Joseph.

"Take Mary as your wife," said the angel. "God has chosen you to take care of her and the child she will bear.

"He will grow up to show God's love and grace to all the world." And Joseph willingly agreed.

ALL THIS HAPPENED long ago, at the time when an emperor in Rome ruled the land. At that time, he sent out messengers with a new command: that everyone must go to their home town, to register their names. Then he could make them pay the tax money he needed to surround himself with power and luxury.

Joseph went to Mary. "My home town is Bethlehem," he said. "We will go there together – for we will soon be family."

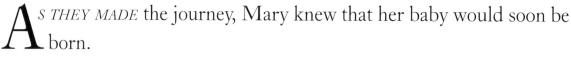

As THEY MADE the journey, Mary knew that her baby would soon be born.

As soon as they arrived, Joseph began searching for a place to stay.

But oh no! The inn was full.

The only place they could shelter was a stable, and there Mary's baby Jesus was born.

She wrapped him in swaddling clothes and laid him in the manger to sleep.

OUT ON THE hills nearby, some shepherds were watching their sheep through the night. They were on the lookout for danger from the shadows…

when suddenly an angel appeared.

"Good news!" cried the angel. "Tonight in Bethlehem a baby has been born!

"He is sent from heaven to show God's love and grace to all the world!
"You will find him wrapped in swaddling clothes and lying in a manger."
And with that the sky was filled with angels singing.

T*HEN AS SUDDENLY* as they had appeared, the sky was dark again.

Had the shepherds been dreaming? Had they really heard those words, that music?

To find out, the shepherds hurried to Bethlehem…

… and found Joseph and Mary and her baby.
Mary listened with wonder and delight as they told her all
that the angel had said.

N OT FAR FROM Bethlehem, in the city of Jerusalem, King Herod paced up and down.

For many years, he had schemed and plotted to gain the power he wielded.

Now strangers from far away had arrived in the city, declaring they had seen signs in the heavens: a star that told them of a newborn king.

Herod's advisors had brought no comfort.

"Our ancient books tell of a king whom God will send to set our people free," they said. "He will be greater than King David of days gone by.

"Like David, he will be born in Bethlehem."

Herod pondered the news, and then he began to scheme.

"I shall send those strangers there to find him," he said.

THE STRANGERS WERE delighted as they set out along the road to Bethlehem. The star that had led them many miles once again lit their way among hills and fields to the little town. There it shone its light on one particular house.

T<small>HEY WENT INSIDE</small> and found Mary
and her child.
Bowing low, they presented their tribute
gifts: gold, frankincense, and myrrh.

T*HAT NIGHT*, in a dream, an angel spoke to them.
"Do not go back to Herod," warned the angel.
"He means to harm the child."
When they awoke and set out for home, they went
a different way.

T*HAT SAME NIGHT*, an angel also spoke to Joseph.

"Get up," whispered the angel. "Danger threatens.
You must take Mary and Jesus far away.

"Do not return to Nazareth until I tell you it is safe."

Joseph gathered his family and set out just as dawn was
breaking.

For Jesus must be kept safe, until the time he would show
God's love and grace to all the world.

Just as the angel had said.

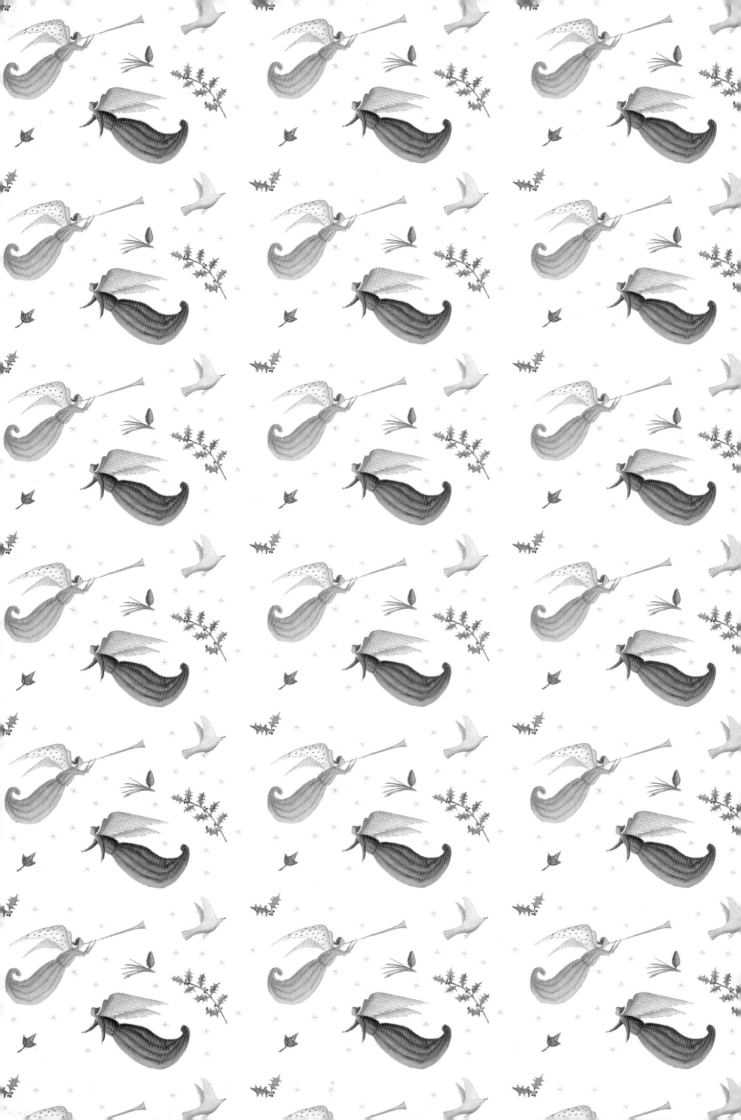